W9-CGM-101

Alex Rodriguez:

A+ Shortstop

by
Mike Shalin

SPORTS PUBLISHING INC.
www.SportsPublishingInc.com

©1999 Sports Publishing Inc.
All rights reserved.

Book design, editor: Susan M. McKinney
Cover design: Scot Muncaster
Photos: *The Associated Press,* Tacoma Rainiers

ISBN: 1-58261-104-1
Library of Congress Catalog Card Number: 99-64072

SPORTS PUBLISHING INC.
SportsPublishingInc.com

Printed in the United States.

CONTENTS

1

it's All on the Web

In this wonderful modern world of fast communications, a kid's favorite baseball team or individual players can be just a few clicks away on the home computer. All teams have their own web sites and the same can be said for some players.

Alex Rodriguez is one of those players with his own site—it's called ARod.com. Call it up and you can read all about the star shortstop's life, read what he has to say and even send him e-mails. It truly is a special place.

But for A-Rod fans, the site was just the place to read more about the bad news that opened the 1999 baseball season for this young star. That was where you could go to read about the left knee injury that knocked Alex out of the first several weeks of the season—the first major injury of his brilliant young career.

You could read about how it happened, how the knee started bothering him when he was jumping over boxes during offseason drills and then got worse near the end of spring training, about how he tried to start the season only to be reminded something was wrong.

You could read about his true feelings on being hurt, about how warm his teammates made him feel when he returned to the dugout—how Ken Griffey Jr. "gave me a big hug and then congratulated me on joining the Mash unit," and later yelled, "you're not somebody until you've been operated on."

The surgery was in no way career threatening, but no one wants to miss basically the first six weeks of the season.

Especially THIS season.

In 1998, Alex became only the third major-leaguer to hit 40 home runs and steal 40 bases in the same season. (AP/Wide World Photos)

Starting a New Club?

It's not that the 1999 campaign was to mean more than any other for this special kid who really loves this game, but there was a buzz about Alex as the season was about to start.

What kind of buzz? Well, in 1998, Alex became only the third player in major league history to enter the 40/40 Club—40 homers and 40 stolen bases in the same season. Jose Canseco was the first to do it, hitting 42 homers and stealing 40 bases for the 1988 Oakland A's. Barry Bonds was next, posting the same numbers for the 1996 San Francisco Giants.

Then came Alex last year—when he hit 42 homers and stole 46 bases for the Mariners.

So, not only had Alex joined this special club, but he had come the closest of the three to starting a NEW club—the 50/50 Club.

In fact, in its preseason edition, *USA Today Baseball Weekly*, running a story headlined "Predicting 1999's best and worst," had a long list of things under the title "Don't be surprised if:" and the first thing on that list read: "Alex Rodriguez becomes the first player to hit 50 HRs and steal 50 bases in a season."

That's a bold prediction, even if it did come under the heading of things that might happen. But people make bold predictions about Alexander Emmanuel Rodriguez, the great young shortstop of the Mariners.

Alex teams with Griffey to form one of the very best 1-2 punches of all-time. But, because the pair plays in Seattle, away from the major media centers, you don't hear as much about Alex as you do about the other great young shortsops—Derek Jeter and Nomar Garciaparra. Playing in New York and Boston has definite advantages, which is why many people believe Alex will leave Seattle after his contract runs out after the 2000 season.

But getting hurt early in the 1999 season made 50/50 look like an unreachable goal—something he'd have to wait to achieve. Missing six weeks could reduce Alex to having to chase the dream of becoming the first player ever to record two 40/40 seasons.

Baseball Weekly *called Alex one of the best players in baseball. (AP/Wide World Photos)*

Small Market Blues

In that same issue of *Baseball Weekly*, a story talked about the sport's Top 10 "Madison Avenue" types, the guys who have the most earning power when it comes to commercials and other off-the-field marketing opportunities.

Griffey was fourth and would have been higher if not for the Seattle market. Alex was listed ninth. "He's another Mariner who could be in Jeter's league (Jeter was No. 7) if he'd only get more national exposure," the story said. "One of the best (if not the best) players in baseball ..."

There you go—one of the best, if not the best players in baseball. Not bad for a 23-year-old kid who fought through some tough financial times growing up to not only become a great player, but also to become the kind of special person who is always helping kids and never forgetting how special it is to play major-league baseball.

After Alex hit a home run on Sept. 19, 1998 to reach the 40/40 club, teammate David Segui, quoted in the *Seattle Post-Intelligencer,* said, "It pretty much reinforces to me that he's the best ballplayer in the game. Definitely, Bonds and Junior (Griffey) are up there with him, but the way he plays the game sets him apart from everyone else, I think he plays the game with the intensity of a fringe player, which is a compliment. He plays the game the way it's supposed to be played, plays to win.

"I'm not alone in this. He's the best in the game. The way he goes about it day in and day out, with a desire to get better—it's very impressive ... let me put it this way: most superstars wouldn't do the things he does."

And, while most players do their part in doing things to help people, no one does more than Alex. When you talk about putting something back into the game, you don't have to look any further than Alex, who learned—from Griffey and others before him—how important it is to act the right way when you're a professional athlete, or any kind of human being. Alex listened well.

Alex was raised by his hard-working mom, Lourdes Navarro. (AP/Wide World Photos)

CHAPTER FOUR

It Wasn't Easy

Alex was born in New York City and his family moved to the Dominican Republic when he was 4 years old. The family lived an affluent lifestyle for a few years, but at age 8, business troubles forced the family to move to Miami, where, a year later, his father left the family never to return.

Alex was basically raised by his hard-working mom and, while other kids ate snacks their family brought them between games of little league double-headers, Alex had no one there because his mom was working.

Alex's mother (left) and friends cheer as Alex talks to the Mariners on draft day, 1993. (AP/Wide World Photos)

That's the story of the young Alex Rodriguez in a nutshell. No, it's not a story of child abuse or beating some rare disease and making it as a ballplayer. But his father leaving—and not getting in touch with Alex again until the day the kid became the first pick in the annual baseball draft— is something that eats at Alex all the time, something that puts the only negative spin on such a positive life.

"Dad left us when I was 9," Alex told the *Seattle Times* in 1998. "What did I know back then? I thought he was coming back. I thought he had gone to the store or something. But he never came back . . . it still hurts."

Alex's dad, Victor, had operated a successful shoe store in New York City but the store wasn't managed properly after the Rodriguez family moved to the Dominican. Then came the move to Miami and the opening of another store.

"From talking with Mom, I found out that Miami wasn't fast-paced enough for Dad, that he wanted to go back to New York and Mom didn't," Alex said in that *Seattle Times* story. "They talked but couldn't agree. So, he split.

"He had been so good to me, actually, spoiled me because I was the baby in the family," Alex said. "I couldn't understand what he had done."

Victor Rodriguez left Alex and his older brother and sister—both already out of high school—with their Mom, Lourdes Navarro, who has since remarried. She worked in a Miami immigration office by day and waited on tables by night—eventually opening her own immigration office—and then a restaurant.

"My Mom is hard-working and smart," Alex said. "As you can see, she is also a good business-woman. I wanted to give her $10,000 once to go away on a great vacation, to rest, to thank her for all she had done for us. She said she would invest the money, instead."

The call from his father came out of the blue, on that June, 1993, day when the Mariners made Alex, still a month short of his 18th birthday, the very first pick of all the amateur baseball players in the country. Just a call, nothing else. It shocked Alex. It angered Lourdes. "My special day, Mom thought, and my father had no right to be a part of it."

Alex thought the call might have been the start of some sort of a reunion. It wasn't.

Then, in 1994, when Alex was preparing to play a winter game in the Dominican Republic, his father showed up. "I was taking batting practice," Alex recalls. "He just bought a ticket and came to the stadium. When this man told me who he was, I almost broke down."

The father and son made plans to meet for lunch the next day. Alex decided not to go. The hurt was too deep. "This was my father, yes," Alex said. "But this was the man who walked away from my mom, who had spent her life working to give us all she could. He had walked away from my brother and my sister, and from me. He had been so good to me before, such a good dad to me, but he walked. I couldn't just go and see him, just like that."

He said he was thinking about doing it some time in the future. He hinted that might be the right thing to do. But the pain of what happened to that 9-year-old boy was just too deep to deal with.

5

Wanting to Help Out

Getting left by his dad at age 9 left deep scars. Alex Rodriguez has turned those scars into positives and is using what happened to him as a kid as an incentive to help other children. He was still too young to have a family of his own—but plenty old enough to do things that can help others, mainly through education.

He works with kids through the Grand Slam for Kids education program in Seattle and authored "Hit a Grand Slam with Alex," which is a motiva-

Alex, who wants to help children, visits the 1999 NikeTown Field Day in Florida. (AP/Wide World Photos)

tional childrens' book aimed at getting kids to think the right way when it comes to education and life's lessons.

"I want to help kids. I want to impress on them the importance of education," Alex says. "I want to have a long and successful baseball career. But when it's done, I want to have another career, teaching civics and coaching basketball."

If you check the A-Rod website, you can find excepts from the book—like: "When I reached school age, I walked out the door eager to learn. I quickly found out Kindergarten would be tougher than I thought." There are other things youngsters can relate to in the book, which also deals with baseball.

Also in the book, Alex says, "without question, the person I looked up to the most was Baltimore shortstop Cal Ripken Jr. I wanted to play shortstop."

Ripken was an idol, but two-time National League Most Valuable Player Dale Murphy is the reason Alex wears No. 3.

This kid has a definite appreciation of those who came before him.

CHAPTER SIX

It Could Have Been Different

You might have caught Alex's previous mention of basketball. Well, he was a pretty fair guard in high school, starting at the point for Miami's Westminster Prep as a freshman.

Back in 1997, Alex was spotted working out with the NBA's Seattle SuperSonics, his ability clear to anyone who was watching.

"Sonics signed me to a 10-day deal, to take them over the hump," he joked to the *Seattle Times.* "I'll call Skip (Mariners manager Lou Piniella) and tell him I'll be a little late for spring training."

Alex says he loves baseball "more than anything except [his] family." (AP/Wide World Photos)

Obviously, he wasn't serious. But that doesn't mean a career in basketball might not have been possible for this gifted athlete. A football career might have happened, too, if baseball hadn't been in the picture.

"I love baseball more than anything except my family," Alex said. "But basketball will always have a special place for me."

Alex thought about starting as a freshman basketball player and recalled, "I was the only one who ever started (as a freshman at the school). I was 6-1 and pretty quick. I played in every game and started some. I must have showed something because I got basketball offers from Florida State, Stetson and Ole Miss."

But his mom had other thoughts. She eliminated basketball from the picture.

"My school was tough scholastically," Alex says. "Mom said I could play only two sports. It was a

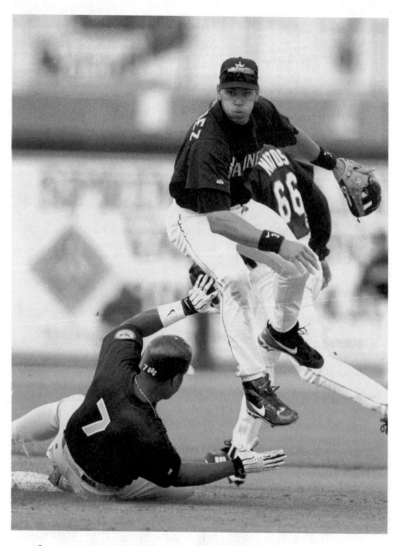

Alex gave up basketball in high school because it ran into the baseball season. (AP/Wide World Photos)

tough choice. I was a pretty good quarterback in football, preseason Parade All-America pick my junior year, before I got hurt. And there was baseball, although back then my basketball was way ahead of my baseball."

The basketball season ran into spring baseball. That was it for basketball.

"It was as if I had baseball in my blood," he says. "Without basketball, I had a chance to work out and be more ready for baseball. Then, as a sophomore, I made a big improvement over my freshman year as a baseball player. Scouts told me if I kept that up, I had a good chance to be a good player and a high draft pick."

That turned out to be a bit of an understatement. Alex became a star and a 17-year-old first pick in the country. The Mariners, still a struggling franchise despite the presence of Griffey—perhaps

Alex and teammate Joey Cora exchange high-fives after being driven in by Ken Griffey, Jr. (AP/Wide World Photos)

the best player in the game at the time — gave Alex a $1 million signing bonus.

"Baseball has worked out well," Alex says. "But I think I could have played some college basketball, maybe Division I."

George Karl, the Sonics' coach at the time, wouldn't argue. "I go to a lot of Mariner games," he said. "The guys who could play our sport are the infielders; quick feet, quick hands. Combine that with Alex's height (he's 6-3, tall for a shortstop), and he just might have had a future in basketball. But I think he's pretty darn good right where he is."

Alex wears No. 3 in honor of former major-league star Dale Murphy. (AP/Wide World Photos)

CHAPTER SEVEN

The Short Trip Begins

For a kid who was born in New York and had moved to the Dominican Republic and Miami by the age of 8, Alex's trip from high school baseball to the major leagues was a relatively easy one.

Yes, he had to learn and make all kinds of adjustments to refine that raw talent—but it took him just three years to go from Westminster Prep to battling for the American League Most Valuable Player Award—and another two years to join that 40/40 Club.

From Wisconsin, Alex moved on to the Double A Jacksonville Suns. (AP/Wide World Photos)

Alex was the first high school player ever invited to try out for Team USA and later in 1993 joined that team, going 4-for-8 in two games for the South Team in the U.S. Olympic Festival in San Antonio before getting nailed in the face by a throw while sitting in the dugout. That forced cosmetic surgery for Alex, who signed his contract with the Mariners on August 30, 1993 but did not play professional baseball that summer.

Alex played in the Arizona Instructional League but batted just .197 (9-for-46) in his brief stay. He did steal six bases and commited just one error in his first taste of professional baseball.

The following season, 1994, Alex played at four different levels in the Seattle system—including, at age 19, his first visit to the major leagues.

His totals for the season were just fine—Alex batted a combined .300, with 21 homers, 86 RBIs and 23 stolen bases in 131 games. And those num-

Alex's last minor-league team was the Tacoma Rainiers.
(Tacoma Rainiers)

bers included the almost predictable .204 in 17 games with the Mariners.

When Alex makes the Hall of Fame, they can go back and look at his first professional team, which was Appleton, Wisconsin—where he hit .319 in the first 65 official games of his professional career. His first professional homer was April 24, 1994 at Fort Wayne and Alex drove in 55 runs in those 65 games before moving on to Double-A Jacksonville, Florida (after being chosen to play in the Midwest League All-Star game, which he had to turn down because of his promotion). He didn't stay in Jacksonville long, either, playing just 17 games (batting .288 in 59 at-bats) before the call came from Seattle July 7.

The first trip to the big leagues wasn't spectacular for Alex, but it wasn't bad, either. On July 8, at Boston's Fenway Park, at the age of 18 years, 11 months and 11 days, he became the first 18 year old since Jose Rijo in 1984 (with the Yankees) to play in the major leagues. He also became just the third 18-year-old shortstop in the major leagues since 1900 (Tony La Russa, 1963, and Robin Yount, 1974 were the others). Alex also became the youngest position player ever to appear in a Mariners uniform (pitcher Edwin Nunez was was a month younger than Alex when he debuted in 1982).

With all the hoopla surrounding his arrival in the big leagues, Alex collected his first major league hit (off Sergio Valdez) and his first stolen base the very next day. He collected his first RBI, at New York, July 16, with a single off Jimmy Key. He went 9-for-34 (.265) in his first 10 games in the majors and was optioned to Triple A Calgary August 2.

In the final month of the minor league season, Alex batted .311 in 32 games, with six homers, 21 RBIs and a couple of stolen bases. He returned for seven more games with the Mariners in September and was later named the organization's Minor League Player of the Year as well as being tabbed the Midwest League's All-Star shortstop and Prospect of the Year.

Alex returned to the Dominican Republic to play winter ball that offseason and would never spend time below the Triple A level again.

Alex split the 1995 season between Tacoma and Seattle. (AP/Wide World Photos)

CHAPTER EIGHT

Seattle, Here He Comes

Alex began the 1995 season at Triple A Tacoma, Washington (the franchise had moved from Calgary). He still hadn't reached his 19th birthday and there was some work to be done. But it was clear the tools were there for this kid to become a very special player.

Alex was recalled from Tacoma on May 6 and batted .333 in 10 games before being sent back to the minors May 27. He was back in the big time again June 8 and started 11 games—hitting his first big-league home run June 12 against Kansas City right-hander Tom Gordon (a three-hit game for Alex). He was back in Tacoma June 23 and called back again July 20. This time, he was shipped back August 15, when Griffey was activated from the disabled list. A-Rod came back to Seattle August 31 and that was basically the end of his days in the minor leagues.

His numbers for 1995? Well, he hit .360 in 54 games with Tacoma—15 homers and 45 RBIs. In his 48 games with the Mariners, Alex batted just .232, with five homers and 19 RBIs. He was named the Triple-A All-Star shortstop by Baseball America and named "Most Exciting Player" and "Best Arm" in the Pacific Coast League in Baseball America's Tools of the Trade special.

Alex arrived at spring training the following February ready to start living up to his potential and all the hype that went along with it. But, as successful as he hoped to be, there was no way even he could have know what was about to take place.

Alex has spent a lot of time working with batting coach Lee Elia. (AP/Wide World Photos)

CHAPTER NINE

A Season for the Ages

Two years before Mark McGwire and Sammy Sosa would capture the hearts and imaginations of baseball fans everywhere, Alex Rodriguez was able to post the kinds of numbers that had to get even the casual baseball fan excited. But first, there was plenty of hard work to be done, a lot of it with Seattle batting coach Lee Elia.

"I have an understanding of what's going on." Alex said during spring training in 1996. "This is not like my first spring—that I'm in awe of the big

In 1996, Alex set the single-season record for extra-base hits by a shortstop. (AP/Wide World Photos)

leagues or something. I'm just trying to get my stuff together."

The Seattle coaches felt Alex's swing might be too long, so they worked with him. "His little finger was over the bat (knob), so we moved that up to give him better bat control. We squared him up (to the plate)," said Elia.

The goal was to get Alex to hit line drives and be able to place the ball wherever the pitch might be. But this was a big jump. As Elia said, "he has to recognize that this is the major leagues. It's not like he goes from AAA (ball) to AAAA."

But the changes had to be made. As Elia would say looking back at the kid's breakout year, "We could see that. He had one asset, bat speed in the hitting area. We waited to see if that would carry him in the majors as it had to the majors. But he was having a rough go of it last spring—still, we waited. He had to want to change." He did. He

Alex (right) poses with teammates Dan Wilson (left), Jay Buhner (second from left) and Edgar Martinez. (AP/World World Photos)

told "Uncle Lee" there was work to do. He had been taking Edgar Martinez hitting tapes home with him to watch—knowing there aren't many better pure hitters than Edgar in the game today.

Eventually, Alex would wind up with an eerily similar hitting style to the one used so well by his teammate. He also was using Griffey's bats. But the swing and the style are Edgar's, a right-handed hitter while Griffey swings from the other side of the plate.

As Martinez said, "Tony Gwynn says (Alex) does Edgar better than Edgar does Edgar."

To which Alex responded: "Why not? "Hasn't Scottie Pippen picked up pointers from Michael Jordan? When you're with the best, you learn from the best."

Learning is one thing. Having a big first full year in the big leagues is another. But having the kind of year Alex had in 1996 is truly incredible.

He played in 141 games for the Mariners—
spending time on the disabled list and two games
back at Tacoma on rehab, in May. He batted a
league-best .358— the highest batting average by a
right-handed hitter since Joe DiMaggio hit .381 in
1939. Alex hit 36 homers, drove in 123 runs and
stole 15 bases. He was named *The Sporting News*
Player of the Year by his peers—in a landslide that
included voting for players in both leagues.

Having turned 21 in July of that season (he hit
his 21st homer of the year on his birthday, July
27), Alex was the third-youngest player ever to win
an American League batting title (trailing only Al
Kaline, 1955, and Ty Cobb, 1907, both 20 when
they won theirs). He was the first shortstop to win
a batting title in 36 years, the first in the AL in 52
years. His batting average was the third-highest ever
by a shortstop and his RBI total was ninth best. He
had 215 hits (91 for extra bases), 54 doubles and

scored 141 runs. He also appeared in his first All-Star game.

Alex became the 11th hitter to make it to the majors by age 20 and go on to win the batting title. The other 10 will all be in the Hall of Fame by the time of George Brett's induction in 1999. Ernie Banks was one of the players, the one who means the most to Alex, "because he was a shortstop."

"I'm only human, so I'm tickled to be mentioned with some of them (like Ty Cobb, Mel Ott and Al Kaline)," Alex said. "But I had a great season—four major-league records for shortstops is mind-boggling."

Truth is he actually had five! The 215 hits, 54 doubles, 91 extra base hits, 141 runs and .631 slugging percentage were all all-time marks for shortstops.

Alex set five records for shortstops in 1996, his first fill season in the majors. (AP/Wide World Photos)

CHAPTER TEN

The Disappointment

When the 1996 season ended—the Mariners having finished out of the playoffs after making it to the postseason the previous year, Alex waited. Many felt he would win the American League Most Valuable Player award. But it didn't happen.

Juan Gonzalez of Texas won the honor in the closest voting since Roger Maris edged Yankee teammate Mickey Mantle in 1960.

"I'm disappointed," Alex admitted from his mother's home in Miami. "I'm happy that Juan won, he's a friend of mine. but to come so close … I wish I had lost by 100 points (he lost by three). Both Seattle writers voting named Griffey as No. 1 on their ballots and one had Alex seventh—thus costing him the distinction of being the youngest MVP in the 65-year history of the award.

"I've got to be honest, I'm hurt a bit, too," Alex said. "It hurts not to get a first-place vote from my own town after the season I had, and that seventh-place vote killed me. But Junior had a big year, too, and he deserved a vote. We help each other out in the lineup."

Alex wanted the award.

"I had trouble sleeping last night, I was getting so psyched up for this," he said. "I thought I had put it out of my mind, tried to tell myself I didn't care that much. But reality struck. I cared a lot."

Said Mariner teammate Martinez: "He may have missed this year, but from what he showed this year he'll have a lot more chances to win MVP."

They may have kept the award away from him, but no one could have taken away the thrills of that special year—that special visit to his first All-Star game, in Philadelphia. He was one of five Mariners who made the American League team that year.

He got the news he was going while his mom and family were visiting in Seattle. He was the youngest shortstop ever to play in the All-Star game and the 15th-youngest player overall to make the game's annual showcase.

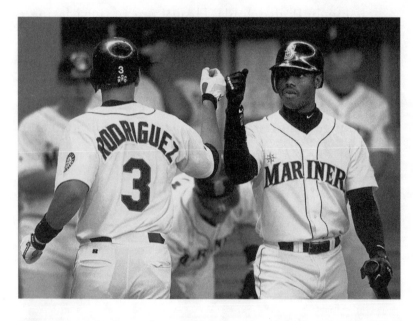

*Alex receives congratulations from teammate Ken Griffey Jr.
after hitting a home run. (AP/Wide World Photos)*

The Quiet Mentor

Ken Griffey Jr. will never be confused with those rah-rah clubhouse leaders who yell and scream to show their leadership. What he is is a superstar, one who leads by performance. But that doesn't mean he turns his back on young players or his team, either.

As soon as a very young Alex Rodriguez arrived in the major leagues, Griffey took the kid under his wing, getting him used to the demands that go along with making it to The Show. If you'd arrive early at a ballpark and the Mariners were out for early batting practice, you would usually find Griffey and Alex together. If you went into the clubhouse, you'd see the same thing, both usually involved in some kind of card game.

Junior would tell you how mature this kid was but that there was a lot to learn.

Obviously, Griffey helped Alex—and all the Mariners—on the field. He's one of the very best players ever and his presence in the lineup, along with potent bats like Martinez and Jay Buhner, made Alex's rise to stardom that much easier.

As he was finishing that monster 1996 season, Alex said he thought Griffey should be the MVP. "What Junior has done for me, does every day for this team, really isn't known," he told the Seattle Times. "How can anyone like me be considered most valuable player in the league when I'm not even the most valuable player in the room?"

Clearly, Alex changed his tune just a bit when the voting was announced. After all, he had finished strong and people were talking about him winning the MVP honor. But Alex's feelings about Junior have always been crystal clear.

"The most obvious thing Junior does for me is get me better pitches," Alex said. "I wouldn't have anywhere close to those numbers if I wasn't hitting in front of him." In fact, Alex was hitting .279 before Piniella moved him in front of Griffey in the Seattle lineup. The rest of the year was one long streak for the young shortstop.

"Alex is having a great season," Piniella said, "...But, let's face it, Junior's our most valuable player day in, day out."

Griffey calls Alex "Young Buck." The two have a special relationship and just might be the best 1-2 punch in the history of the game by the time they are finished with their careers.

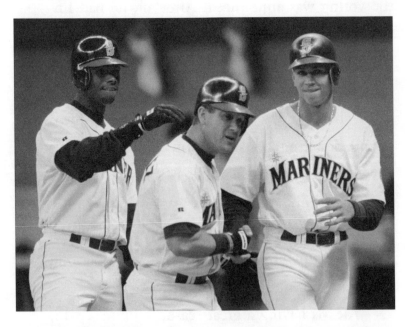

Alex and Ken Griffey, Jr., shown here with teammate Edgar Martinez, have a special relationship. (AP/Wide World Photos)

12

A Tough Act to Follow

You look at Alex's numbers from 1996 and you wonder what this guy could ever do to even come close to equaling that incredible year.

"Baseball expectations and pressures are so great, it's reality," Mark McGwire told the Seattle Times late in the 1996 season—McGwire having hit 49 homers in his rookie season and knowing all about pressure even in '96—two seasons before his historic home run chase. "I only had to carry it for home runs. (Alex) has to carry it for average, home runs and RBIs. But from everyone I've talked to who knows him, he's so well-rounded and so level-headed, they really believe he can do it. I hope the best for him for 20 more years."

Alex's knowledge and appreciation of the game —and the words of his mom, who was always keeping him in his place—allowed him to keep that level head McGwire talked about. "I've talked to Jose (Canseco) for four, five hours about life and expecatations," Alex said back then. "I've talked to Junior, Ripken. I can't expect to hit .358 every year or hit 36 home runs, but one thing I can expect of myself is to stay healthy, play every day, be consistent, and the numbers will be there."

Added McGwire: "It's an unbelievable year. He probably exceeded anybody's expectations as to how well he did. He's absolutely exciting to watch from the (opposing) players bench.

"I was talking to a friend on the PGA Tour and wanted to see what he thought of Tiger Woods. He said, 'You only see a guy who has it all come along like this every 10 to 15 years or so.' I'd put Alex in that same category. I can't think of anyone who has done what he has done."

Elia, his batting coach, saw no reason why Alex wouldn't keep the big numbers going in 1997. "What did he do the second time around the league last year?" Elia asked. "He hit better than he did the first half. Alex has quickness and sound mechanics. Quickness helps you hit the fastball, mechanics, like keeping the hands back, help you hit everything else they throw."

Alex compared his first year to Miami football hero Dan Marino. "He had a great first season, He followed that with a great career," Alex said, hoping to change one thing about his own career in

comparison to Marino's—by winning champion-
ships.

"I'd take less (numbers), with a championship
or two," Alex said. "I know Marino would, because
he told me one day that it hurts him to have gone
to the Super Bowl that first year and not get back.
He said, 'all you want to do is win.' "

And that's what Alex has always heard when
he's talked to the greats of his own game—guys like
Ripken. "All they talk about is the team winning,"
Alex says. "They don't talk about personal numbers. Numbers are overrated."

Good But Not '96 Great

The people who wondered what Alex could do for an encore after 1996 turned out to be right. It wasn't that Alex had a bad year in 1997—but he didn't come close to posting the numbers he had run up the previous year. For most guys, 1997 would have been considered a success. For Alex, it was a pretty good year—he hit .300 with 23 homers, 84 RBIs and 29 stolen bases while going to his second straight All-Star game (he was the first American League player to start at

Alex turns the double play at second. (AP/Wide World Photos)

shortstop besides Ripken since 1983) and helping the Mariners into the American League playoffs.

Alex did become only the third Mariner (Ruppert Jones and Phil Bradley were the others) to join the 20/20 Club, which he would leave in the dust in 1998. He became the second Mariner ever to hit for the cycle when he did it June 5 at Detroit—thus winning $1 million for a Washington native in a radio contest. In the playoffs, he went 5-for-16 with a home run in the loss to the Baltimore Orioles. All good numbers—but not 1996 numbers.

Alex was chosen as a member of the 1998 Associated Press All-Star Team. (AP/Wide World Photos)

Joining The Club

After having hired a personal trainer and improving his own work habits, Alex moved back into the big-number neighborhood in 1998. No, he didn't hit .358. He had to settle for a mere .310—but he belted those 42 homers, drove in 124 runs, had 213 hits, scored 123 runs and stole the 46 bases.

Seattle broadcaster Dave Henderson, who played with Canseco when Jose was the first 40/40 player, marvels at Alex. "People used to talk about

In 1998, Alex hit .310 with 42 homers and 124 RBIs. (AP/Wide World Photos)

'five-tool' players," Henderson said. "This puts it way beyond the five-tool player. Once the league adjusted to Alex, he made his own adjustments. That signifies greatness. There's no fluke in this man's game."

But there is that desire to get better and better—his tireless work allowing him to join Canseco and Bonds in that very special club. "It's just a great lesson for me as a young player about the necessity of hard work," he said after the '98 season. "That's what I attribute my success to (in '98), all my work. It's probably the thing I'm most proud of, more than being the batting champion (in '96). This is something I'm very, very proud of, something I'll never forget."

The 46 stolen bases really were a marked improvement over his brief past in the game. The quickness was always there, but the steals weren't. "He's very fast, quick and he's just a great athlete," says former teammate Rich Amaral, a three-time 50-steals guy in the minors who worked with Alex on the art of swiping bases. "He's got great instincts. I think the one thing he probably didn't realize is how many opportunities you'll come across over the course of a year, if you're looking for them and playing every day like he does.

"I love talking to him about base stealing. I love researching the pitchers and I would go over their quickness to the plate, what they threw, tendancies. It was exciting for me to have him so excited about that aspect of the game."

Alex also talked to all-time base stealing king Rickey Henderson about the craft and Dave Henderson provided his words of wisdom, too. "He's an outstanding ballplayer, but he's a tremendous learner," Dave Henderson said. "We spent time talking about base stealing, and he put it together and learned something. He wants to learn and be the best he can be."

15

It Was All for Nothing

Alex was thrilled to post the numbers he was able to reach in 1998—but hardly thrilled with the way the season went for the Mariners. With the team in the middle of a contract problem with ace pitcher Randy Johnson, things just never went right. Johnson struggled and was eventually traded to the Houston Astros when it was clear Seattle was going straight to nowhere.

This drove Alex crazy.

"Never—not in baseball, basketball or football, not in prep or pro, never in my life, have I been on

Alex was frustrated by his team's struggles in 1998.
(AP/Wide World Photos)

a team in this position," Alex told the *Seattle Times* in September, 1998. "It's a horrible feeling.

"It's hard to explain how I've felt all year, about a situation like this. You can't go hide. It's wrong to (complain). You can only be a man and try to win each game each day. You take notes, you remember, and when you get the chance someday, you pay back the teams that are pounding on you now."

He just didn't accept losing very well. He had been on divison winners in 1995 and '97 and been eliminated on the final weekend of 1996. He was used to having something to play for in September. But not in 1998.

"I'm thinking about this 24 hours a day," he said at the time. "My whole life is baseball. I keep trying to find a way to win. You're aware of that fine line they talk about between trying too hard, taking on too much yourself. But I'll do anything to win. I'll even cheat to win."

It was so bad the approaching 40/40 wasn't as big a deal as it might have been—Alex even saying, "I'll take my 20/20 from last year if the team can have 20 more wins than we do." Twenty more wins would have done it, but it wasn't going to happen in this down year—and Johnson's departure and the continued pitching woes made the future for the Mariners anything but bright, even with a new stadium opening in the summer of 1999.

But through all the losing of 1998, Alex vowed to play like the games really meant something. Every game is a challenge, every game is worth winning.

"I'm trying to play with integrity and pride, trying to show leadership in that way," he said. "I'll keep my head up and I won't let our situation compromise my work. I'll go out every day and do my work and perform as hard as I can, as if we were sitting in first place."

CHAPTER SIXTEEN

This is What Makes A-Rod So Special

Being the best at what he does is the most important thing in Alex's life— unless you count how hard he works at getting kids to be all they can be, or the best person HE can be off the field. He won't accept anything else. He has friends who feel the same way he does—Yankee shortstop Derek Jeter —who is just like Alex, is one of his best friends—and there's always Mom there at every turn to tell him what he's doing right and wrong.

"My mom says fame and money mean nothing if you don't stay the same person you were," Alex says. "I won't ever forget when she was working two jobs to support us—Suzy, Joe, me. You forget these things, you forget who you are."

Alex isn't about to forget who he is (neither is anyone else in the baseball world, for that matter). He is not about to forget one of his basic philosophies, which deals with being humble and what it means when it comes to how other people see you.

"You establish yourself in this game in-out," Alex said at the All-Star game in 1997. "You don't establish yourself out-in, meaning endorsements first and all that stuff. I think I started with a good foundation. I think my humility helped, obviously.

"You don't want to come into this game talking and saying all the wrong things and disrespecting the game. That's number one. I think this game

Alex and Ivan Rodriguez celebrate after scoring in the
1998 All-Star Game. (AP/Wide World Photos)

of baseball needs good people. It needs good personalities. This game needs so much help."

It wouldn't if there were more people like Lourdes Navarro's son, Alex.

People talk about the great players being leaders and Alex answers by saying he'll lead "Essentially, by performance. By pushing others as Jay (Buhner) pushed me, as Junior pushed me.

"Leadership is a role you have to earn in order to be effective. Those other guys, along with Edgar, have been our leaders, and I think I can help them in a collective sense."

Said Martinez: "You don't declare yourself a leader. You show it with what you do, and Alex does it. He has the qualities and he is respected."

And, remember, Alex Rodriguez was still only 23 when the 1999 baseball season began.

Alex Rodriguez's career stats through 1998

YEAR	CLUB	AVG.	G	AB	R	H	2B	3B	HR	RBI	BB	SO	SB
1994	Appleton	.319	65	248	49	79	17	6	14	55	24	44	16
	Jacksonville	.288	17	59	7	17	4	1	1	8	10	13	2
	Seattle	.204	17	54	4	11	0	0	0	2	3	20	3
	Calgary	.311	32	119	22	37	7	4	6	21	8	25	2
1995	Tacoma	.360	54	214	37	77	12	3	15	45	18	44	2
	Seattle	.232	48	142	15	33	6	2	5	19	6	42	4
1996	Seattle	.358	146	601	14	12	15	54	1	36	12	35	9
	Tacoma	.200	2	5	0	1	0	0	0	0	2	1	0
1997	Seattle	.300	141	587	100	176	40	3	23	84	41	99	29
1998	Seattle	.310	161	686	123	213	35	5	42	124	45	121	46
Major League Totals		.313	513	2070	383	648	135	11	106	352	154	386	97

Division Series

1995	Sea vs NY	.000	1	1	1	0	0	0	0	0	0	0	0
1997	Sea vs. NY	.313	4	16	1	5	1	0	1	1	0	5	0
Totals		.294	5	17	2	5	1	0	1	1	0	5	0

League Championship Series

1995	Sea vs. Cle	.000	1	1	0	0	0	0	0	0	0	1	0

All-Star Game

1996	@ Phila	.000	1	1	0	0	0	0	0	0	0	0	0
1997	@ Cle	.333	1	3	0	1	0	0	0	0	0	2	0
1998	@ Col	.667	1	3	2	2	0	0	1	1	0	1	0
Totals		.429	3	7	2	3	0	0	1	1	0	3	0

Major League Shortsops with 35+ Homers

HR	Year	Player, club	Age
47	1958	Ernie Banks, Cubs	27
45	1959	Ernie Banks, Cubs	28
44	1955	Ernie Banks, Cubs	24
43	1957	Ernie Banks, Cubs	26
42	1998	Alex Rodriguez, Mariners	22
41	1960	Ernie Banks, Cubs	29
40	1969	Rico Petrocelli, Red Sox	26
39	1949	Vern Stephens, Red Sox	28
36	1996	Alex Rodriguez, Marinners	21
35	1998	Nomar Garciaparra, RedSox	25

Youngest players with 35+ Homers in one season

Player	Year	Age
Mel Ott	1929	20.184
Frank Robinson	1956	21.000
Alex Rodriguez	1996	21.036
Eddie Matthews	1953	21.299
Hal Trotsky	1934	21.323

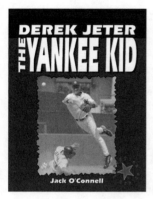

Derek Jeter: The Yankee Kid

Author: Jack O'Connell
ISBN: 1-58261-043-6

In 1996 Derek burst onto the scene as one of the most promising young shortstops to hit the big leagues in a long time. His hitting prowess and ability to turn the double play have definitely fulfilled the early predictions of greatness.

A native of Kalamazoo, MI, Jeter has remained well grounded. He patiently signs autographs and takes time to talk to the young fans who will be eager to read more about him in this book.

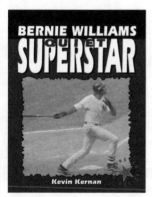

Bernie Williams: Quiet Superstar

Author: Kevin Kernan
ISBN: 1-58261-044-4

Bernie Williams, a guitar-strumming native of Puerto Rico, is not only popular with his teammates, but is considered by top team officials to be the heir to DiMaggio and Mantle fame.

He draws frequent comparisons to Roberto Clemente, perhaps the greatest player ever from Puerto Rico. Like Clemente, Williams is humble, unassuming, and carries himself with quiet dignity. Also like Clemente, he plays with rare determination and a special elegance. He's married, and serves as a role model not only for his three children, but for his young fans here and in Puerto Rico.

Ken Griffey, Jr.:
The Home Run Kid
Author: Larry Stone
ISBN: 1-58261-041-x

Capable of hitting majestic home runs, making breathtaking catches, and speeding around the bases to beat the tag by a split second, Ken Griffey, Jr. is baseball's Michael Jordan. Amazingly, Ken reached the Major Leagues at age 19, made his first All-Star team at 20, and produced his first 100 RBI season at 21.

The son of Ken Griffey, Sr., Ken is part of the only father-son combination to play in the same outfield together in the same game, and, like Barry Bonds, he's a famous son who turned out to be a better player than his father.

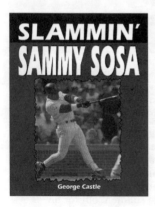

Sammy Sosa:
Slammin' Sammy
Author: George Castle
ISBN: 1-58261-029-0

1998 was a break-out year for Sammy as he amassed 66 home runs, led the Chicago Cubs into the playoffs and finished the year with baseball's ultimate individual honor, MVP.

When the national spotlight was shone on Sammy during his home run chase with Mark McGwire, America got to see what a special person he is. His infectious good humor and kind heart have made him a role model across the country.

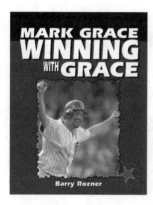

Mark Grace:
Winning with Grace
Author: Barry Rozner
ISBN: 1-58261-056-8

This southern California native and San Diego State alumnus has been playing baseball in the windy city for nearly fifteen years. Apparently the cold hasn't affected his game. Mark is an all-around player who can hit to all fields and play great defense.

Mark's outgoing personality has allowed him to evolve into one of Chicago's favorite sons. He is also community minded and some of his favorite charities include the Leukemia Society of America and Easter Seals.

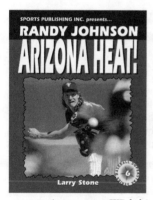

Randy Johnson:
Arizona Heat!
Author: Larry Stone
ISBN: 1-58261-042-8

One of the hardest throwing pitchers in the Major Leagues, and, at 6'10" the tallest, the towering figure of Randy Johnson on the mound is an imposing sight which strikes fear into the hearts of even the most determined opposing batters.

Perhaps the most amazing thing about Randy is his consistency in recording strikeouts. He is one of only four pitchers to lead the league in strikeouts for four consecutive seasons. With his recent signing with the Diamondbacks, his career has been rejuvenated and he shows no signs of slowing down.

Omar Vizquel:
The Man with the Golden Glove

Author: Dennis Manoloff
ISBN: 1-58261-045-2

Omar has a career fielding percentage of .982 which is the highest career fielding percentage for any shortstop with at least 1,000 games played.

Omar is a long way from his hometown of Caracas, Venezuela, but his talents as a shortstop put him at an even greater distance from his peers while he is on the field.

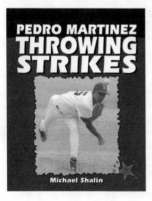

Pedro Martinez:
Throwing Strikes

Author: Mike Shalin
ISBN: 1-58261-047-9

The 1997 National League Cy Young Award winner is always teased because of his boyish looks. He's sometimes mistaken for the batboy, but his curve ball and slider leave little doubt that he's one of the premier pitchers in the American League.

It is fitting that Martinez is pitching in Boston, where the passion for baseball runs as high as it does in his native Dominican Republic.

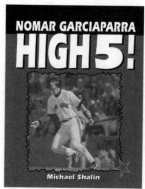

Nomar Garciaparra: High 5!

Author: Mike Shalin
ISBN: 1-58261-053-3

An All-American at Georgia Tech, a star on the 1992 U.S. Olympic Team, the twelfth overall pick in the 1994 draft, and the 1997 American League Rookie of the Year, Garciaparra has exemplified excellence on every level.

At shortstop, he'll glide deep into the hole, stab a sharply hit grounder, then throw out an opponent on the run. At the plate, he'll uncoil his body and deliver a clutch double or game-winning homer. Nomar is one of the game's most complete players.

Juan Gonzalez: Juan Gone!

Author: Evan Grant
ISBN: 1-58261-048-7

One of the most prodigious and feared sluggers in the major leagues, Gonzalez was a two-time home run king by the time he was 24 years old.

After having something of a personal crisis in 1996, the Puerto Rican redirected his priorities and now says baseball is the third most important thing in his life after God and family.

Mo Vaughn:
Angel on a Mission

Author: Mike Shalin
ISBN: 1-58261-046-0

Growing up in Connecticut, this Angels slugger learned the difference between right and wrong and the value of honesty and integrity from his parents early on, lessons that have stayed with him his whole life.

This former American League MVP was so active in Boston charities and youth programs that he quickly became one of the most popular players ever to don the Red Sox uniform.

Mo will be a welcome addition to the Angels line-up and the Anaheim community.

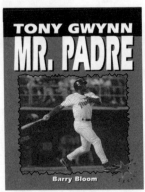

Tony Gwynn:
Mr. Padre

Author: Barry Bloom
ISBN: 1-58261-049-5

Tony is regarded as one of the greatest hitters of all-time. He is one of only three hitters in baseball history to win eight batting titles (the others: Ty Cobb and Honus Wagner).

In 1995 he won the Branch Rickey Award for Community Service by a major leaguer. He is unfailingly humble and always accessible, and he holds the game in deep respect. A throwback to an earlier era, Gwynn makes hitting look effortless, but no one works harder at his craft.

Kevin Brown:
That's Kevin with a "K"

Author: Jacqueline Salman
ISBN: 1-58261-050-9

Kevin was born in McIntyre, Georgia and played college baseball for Georgia Tech. Since then he has become one of baseball's most dominant pitchers and when on top of his game, he is virtually unhittable.

Kevin transformed the Florida Marlins and San Diego Padres into World Series contenders in consecutive seasons, and now he takes his winning attitude and talent to the Los Angeles Dodgers.

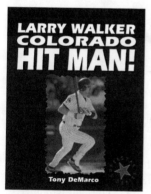

Larry Walker:
Colorado Hit Man!

Author: Tony DeMarco
ISBN: 1-58261-052-5

Growing up in Canada, Larry had his sights set on being a hockey player. He was a skater, not a slugger, but when a junior league hockey coach left him off the team in favor of his nephew, it was hockey's loss and baseball's gain.

Although the Rockies' star is known mostly for his hitting, he has won three Gold Glove awards, and has worked hard to turn himself into a complete, all-around ballplayer. Larry became the first Canadian to win the MVP award.

Sandy and Roberto Alomar:
Baseball Brothers

Author: Barry Bloom
ISBN: 1-58261-054-1

Sandy and Roberto Alomar are not just famous baseball brothers they are also famous baseball sons. Sandy Alomar, Sr. played in the major leagues fourteen seasons and later went into management. His two baseball sons have made names for themselves and have appeared in multiple All-Star games.

With Roberto joining Sandy in Cleveland, the Indians look to be a front-running contender in the American League Central.

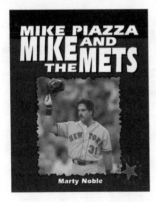

Mike Piazza:
Mike and the Mets

Author: Marty Noble
ISBN: 1-58261-051-7

A total of 1,389 players were selected ahead of Mike Piazza in the 1988 draft, who wasn't picked until the 62nd round, and then only because Tommy Lasorda urged the Dodgers to take him as a favor to his friend Vince Piazza, Mike's father.

Named in the same breath with great catchers of another era like Bench, Dickey and Berra, Mike has proved the validity of his father's constant reminder "If you work hard, dreams do come true."

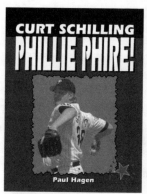

Curt Schilling: Phillie Phire!

Author: Paul Hagen
ISBN: 1-58261-055-x

Born in Anchorage, Alaska, Schilling has found a warm reception from the Philadelphia Phillies faithful. He has amassed 300+ strikeouts in the past two seasons and even holds the National League record for most strikeouts by a right handed pitcher at 319.

This book tells of the difficulties Curt faced being traded several times as a young player, and how he has been able to deal with off-the-field problems.

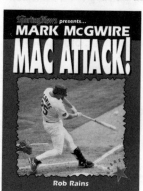

Mark McGwire: Mac Attack!

Author: Rob Rains
ISBN: 1-58261-004-5

Mac Attack! describes how McGwire overcame poor eyesight and various injuries to become one of the most revered hitters in baseball today. He quickly has become a legendary figure in St. Louis, the home to baseball legends such as Stan Musial, Lou Brock, Bob Gibson, Red Schoendienst and Ozzie Smith. McGwire thought about being a police officer growing up, but he hit a home run in his first Little League at-bat and the rest is history.

Roger Clemens: Rocket Man!

Author: Kevin Kernan
ISBN: 1-58261-128-9

Alex Rodriguez: A-plus Shortstop

ISBN: 1-58261-104-1

Baseball
SuperStar Series Titles

Collect Them All!

____ Sandy and Roberto Alomar: Baseball Brothers

____ Kevin Brown: Kevin with a "K"

____ Roger Clemens: Rocket Man!

____ Juan Gonzalez: Juan Gone!

____ Mark Grace: Winning With Grace

____ Ken Griffey, Jr.: The Home Run Kid

____ Tony Gwynn: Mr. Padre

____ Derek Jeter: The Yankee Kid

____ Randy Johnson: Arizona Heat!

____ Pedro Martinez: Throwing Strikes

____ Mike Piazza: Mike and the Mets

____ Alex Rodriguez: A-plus Shortstop

____ Curt Schilling: Philly Phire!

____ Sammy Sosa: Slammin' Sammy

____ Mo Vaughn: Angel on a Mission

____ Omar Vizquel: The Man with a Golden Glove

____ Larry Walker: Colorado Hit Man!

____ Bernie Williams: Quiet Superstar

____ Mark McGwire: Mac Attack!

Available by calling 877-424-BOOK